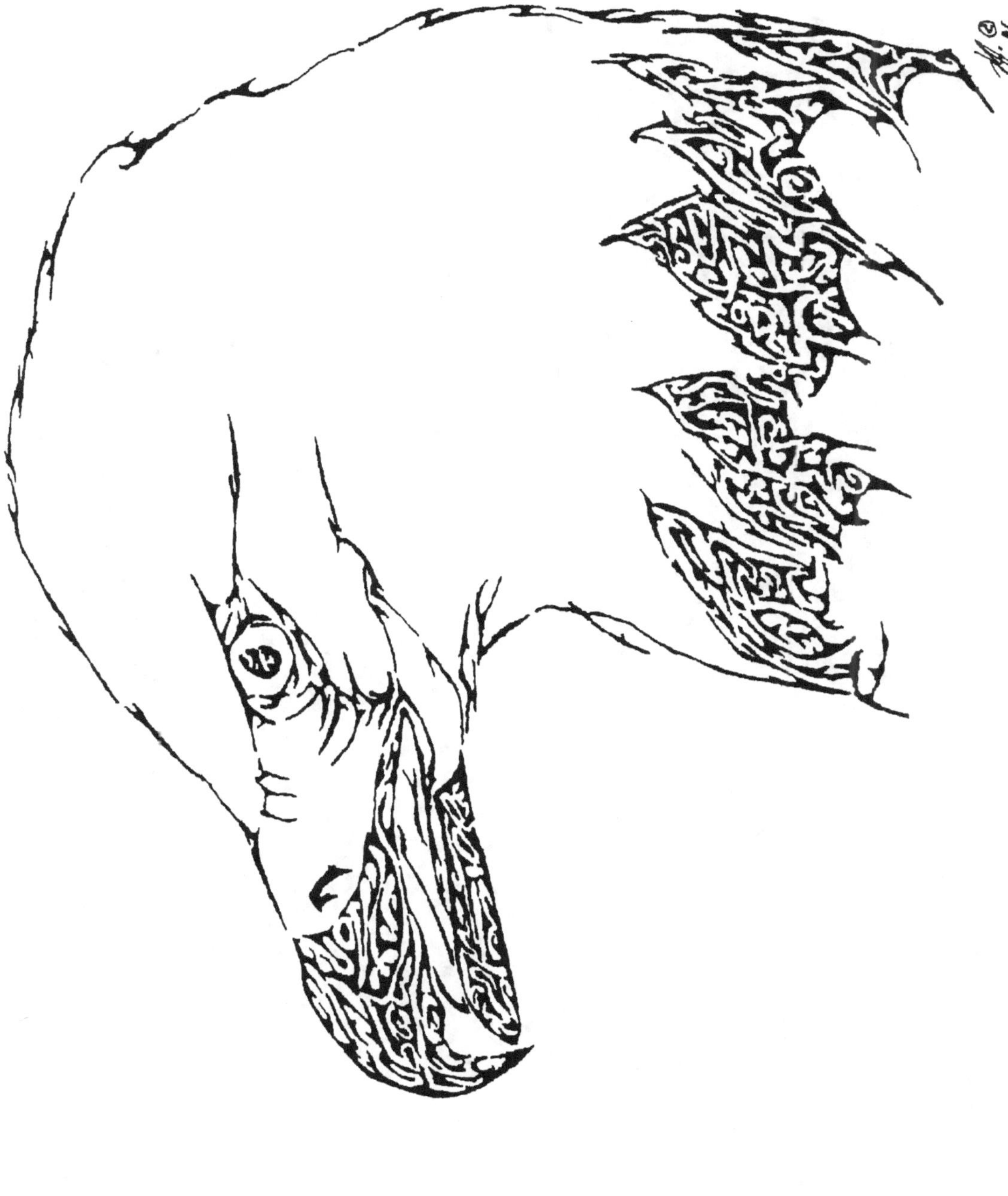

During my first trip to Alaska I was so inspired by its beauty I created a series of artwork. My hope is that you will find the images as beautiful as I, while creating them.

My art style was inspired by the old method of creating silk screens over 25 years ago. Depending on your background, culture, or mind set, you might see something completely different within each image. You may even notice a different image than what I actually intended, finding wonderful hidden treasures within each piece itself.

It is amazing that we can create such incredible images out of different parts and pieces. That our minds can connect individual lines and merge them into amazing ensembles of art. As my style continued to develop, it became the way I see the energy and flow of the world. An under lying base of life. People have seen many different cultural and artistic influences from around the world in my art. When colored, it can take on the look of stained glass. It makes my heart warm when I hear all the different things people see in my style.

You will find many of the pieces emphasize negative space. In each image the negative space is just as important as the positive space. When coloring, allow yourself to explore both inside and outside the lines with a variety of hues. Let the colors flow naturally, in a way that feels right to you. There is no wrong or right way to color.

The last page has all art listed with what the main image is of. But don't look at it until you decide what each art piece is first. Because you might see something very different and that is wonderful.

Each page can be cut cut and framed so you can display your colored creations.

The art is printed on one side of the paper.

Recommend using cardstock or multiple sheets of paper to stop bleed-through to the next page. You can test on the last few pages in the book.

Happy coloring,

Brian Scott

ISBN: 1523886765 ISBN-13: 978-1523886760

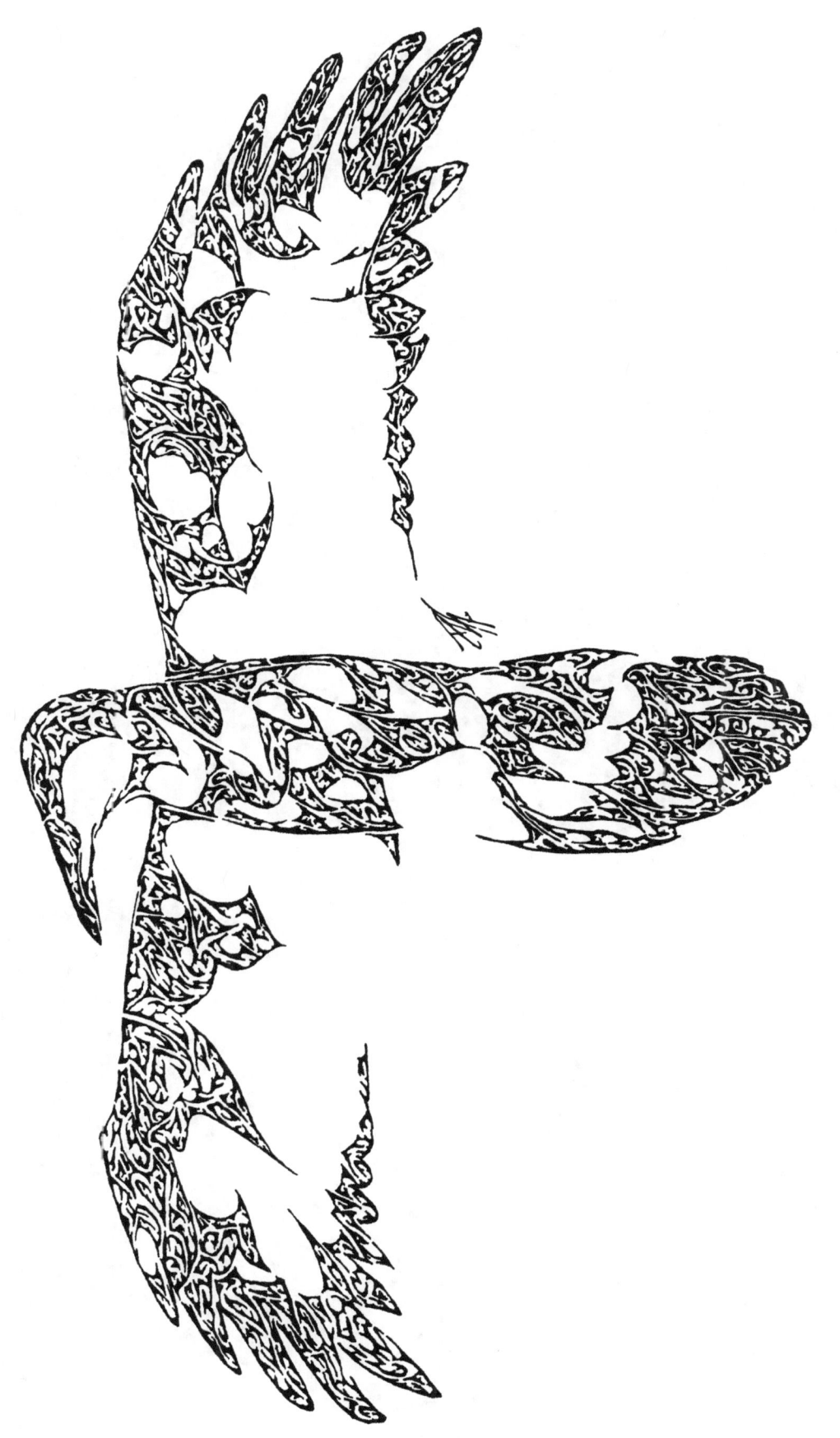

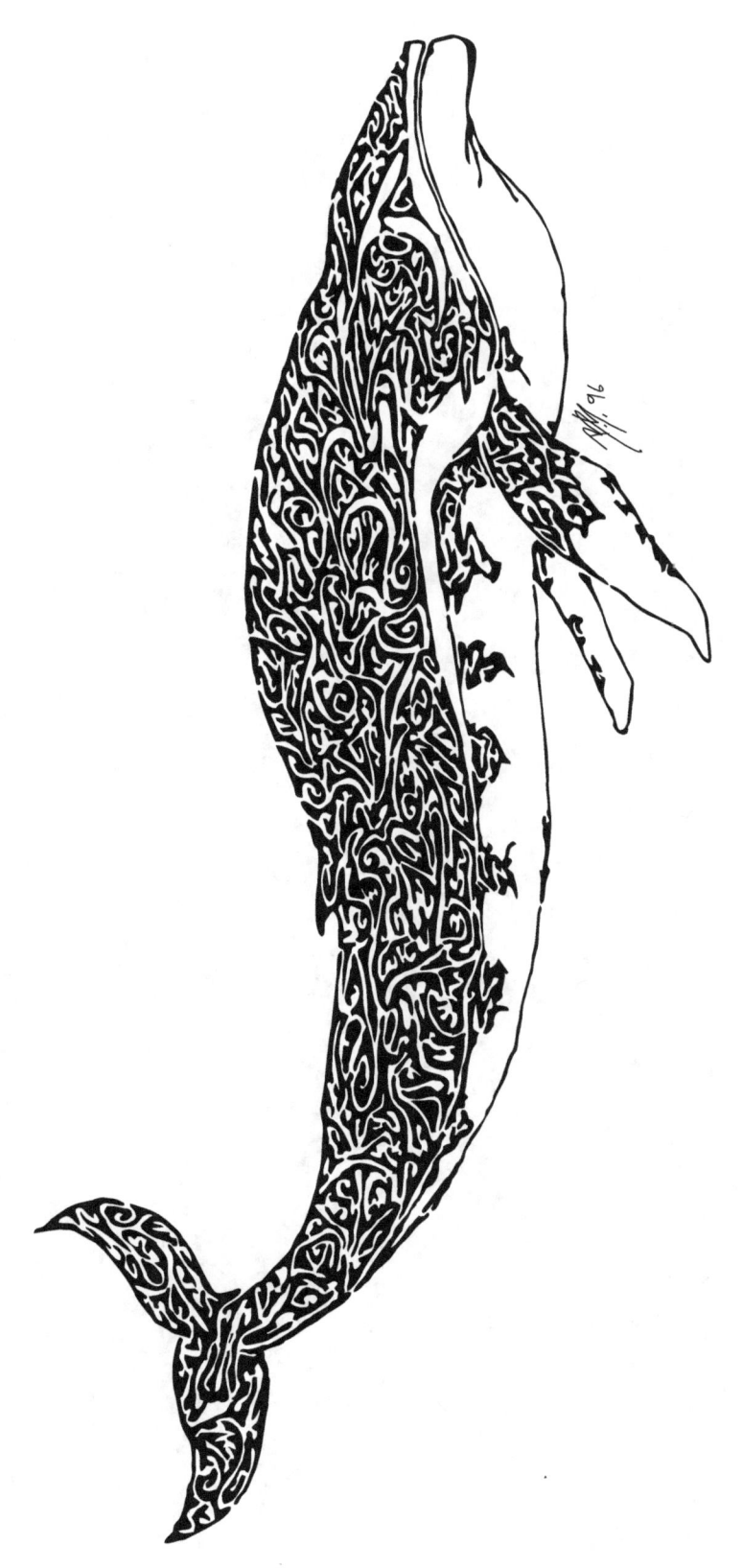

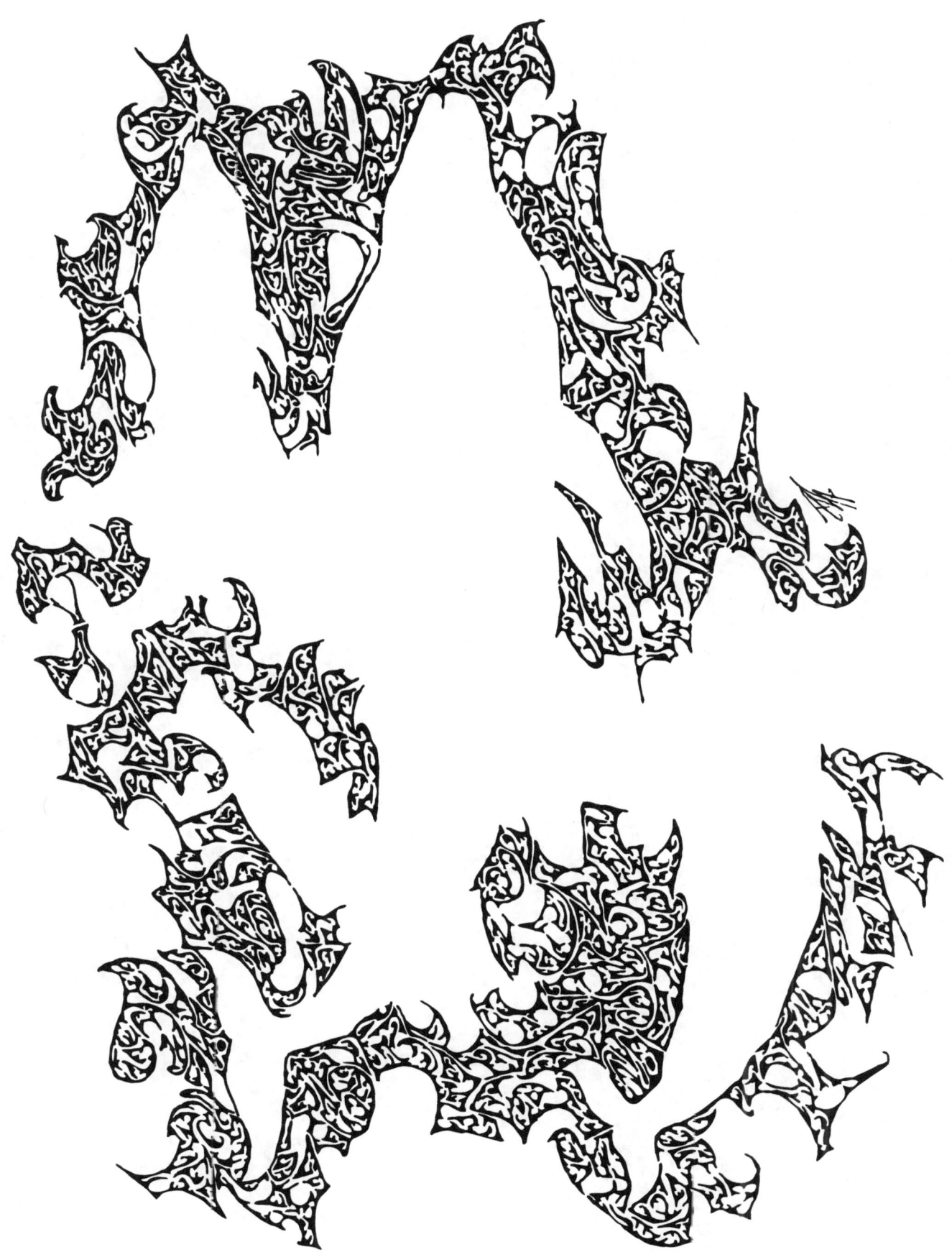

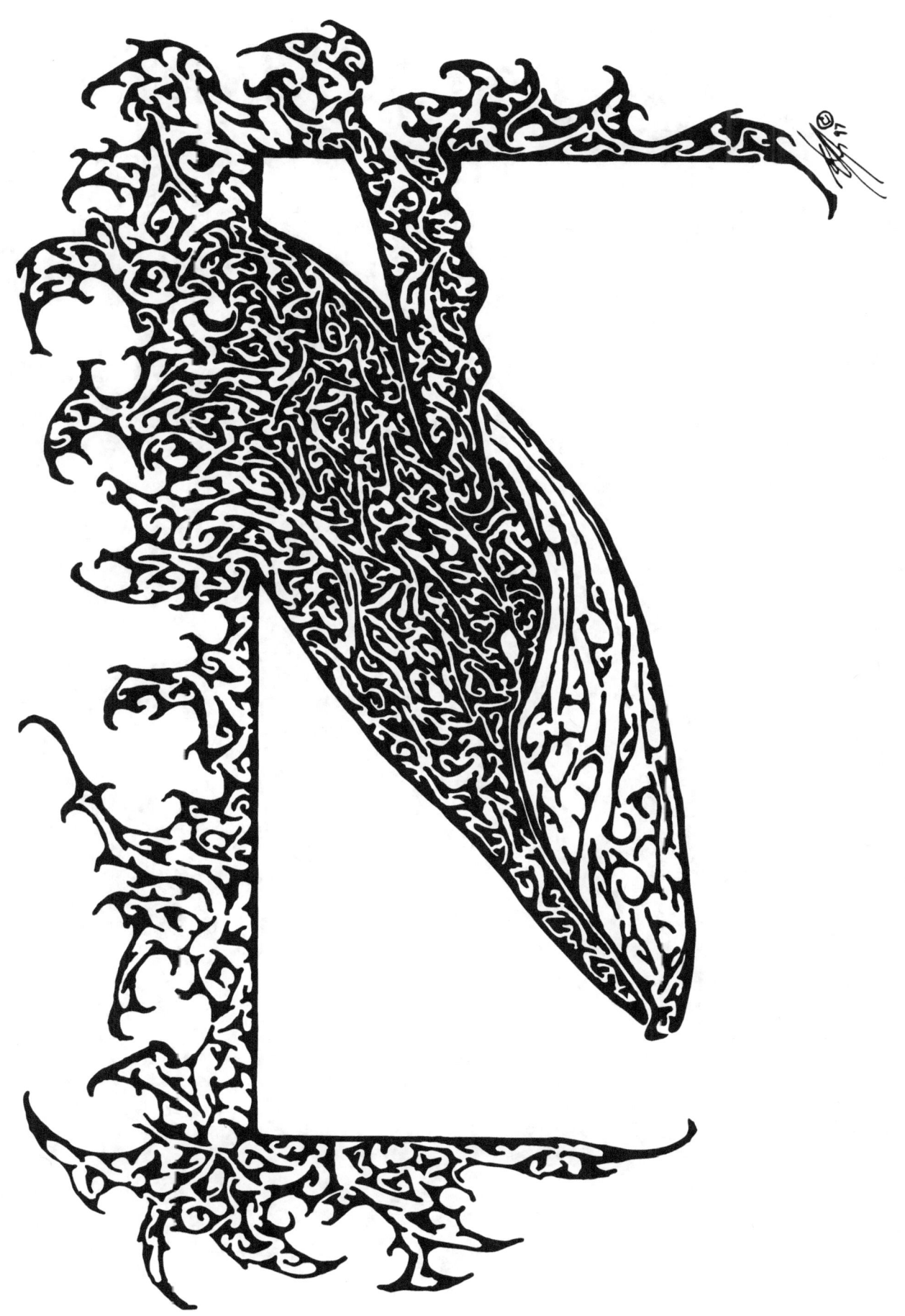

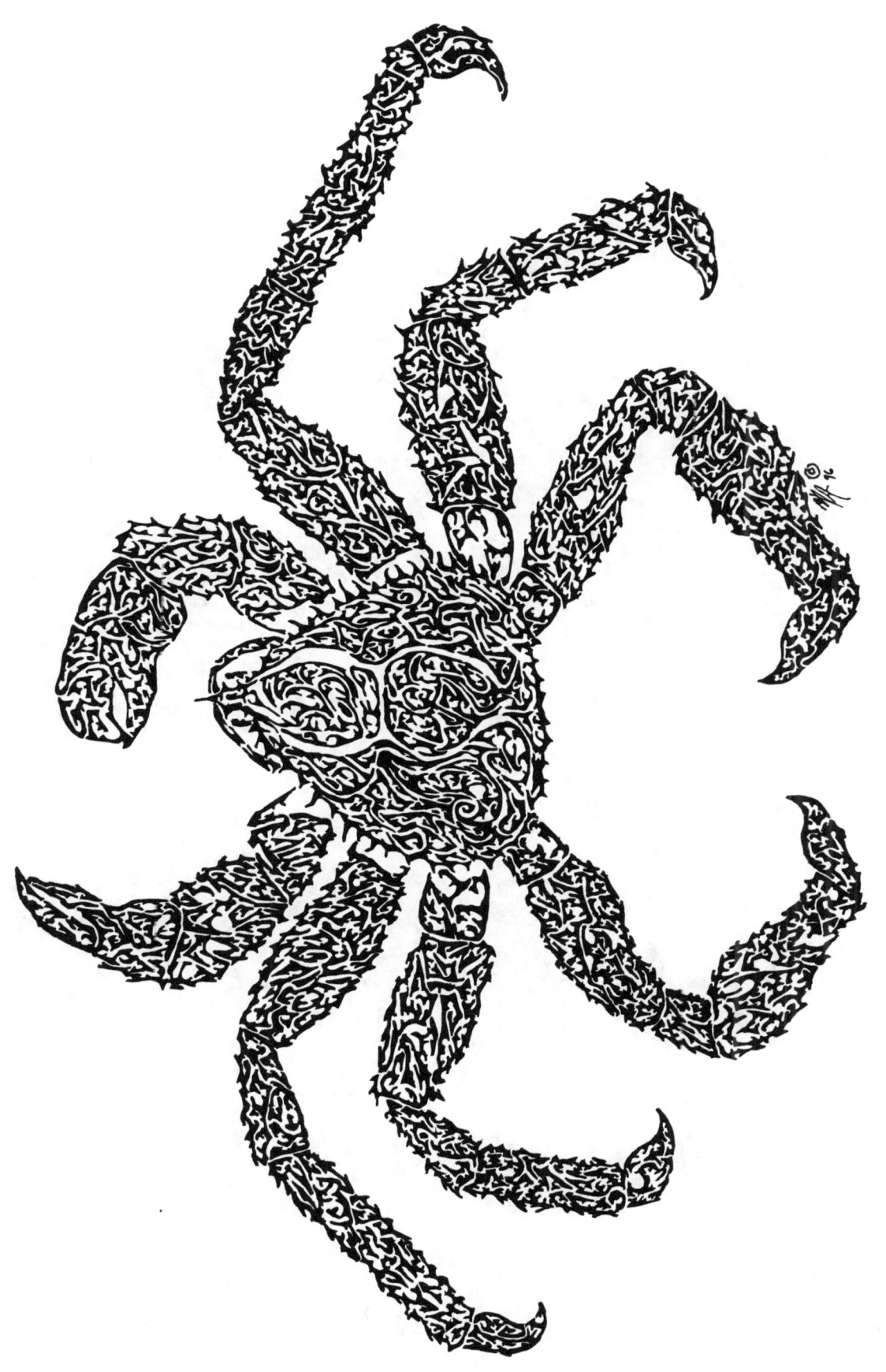

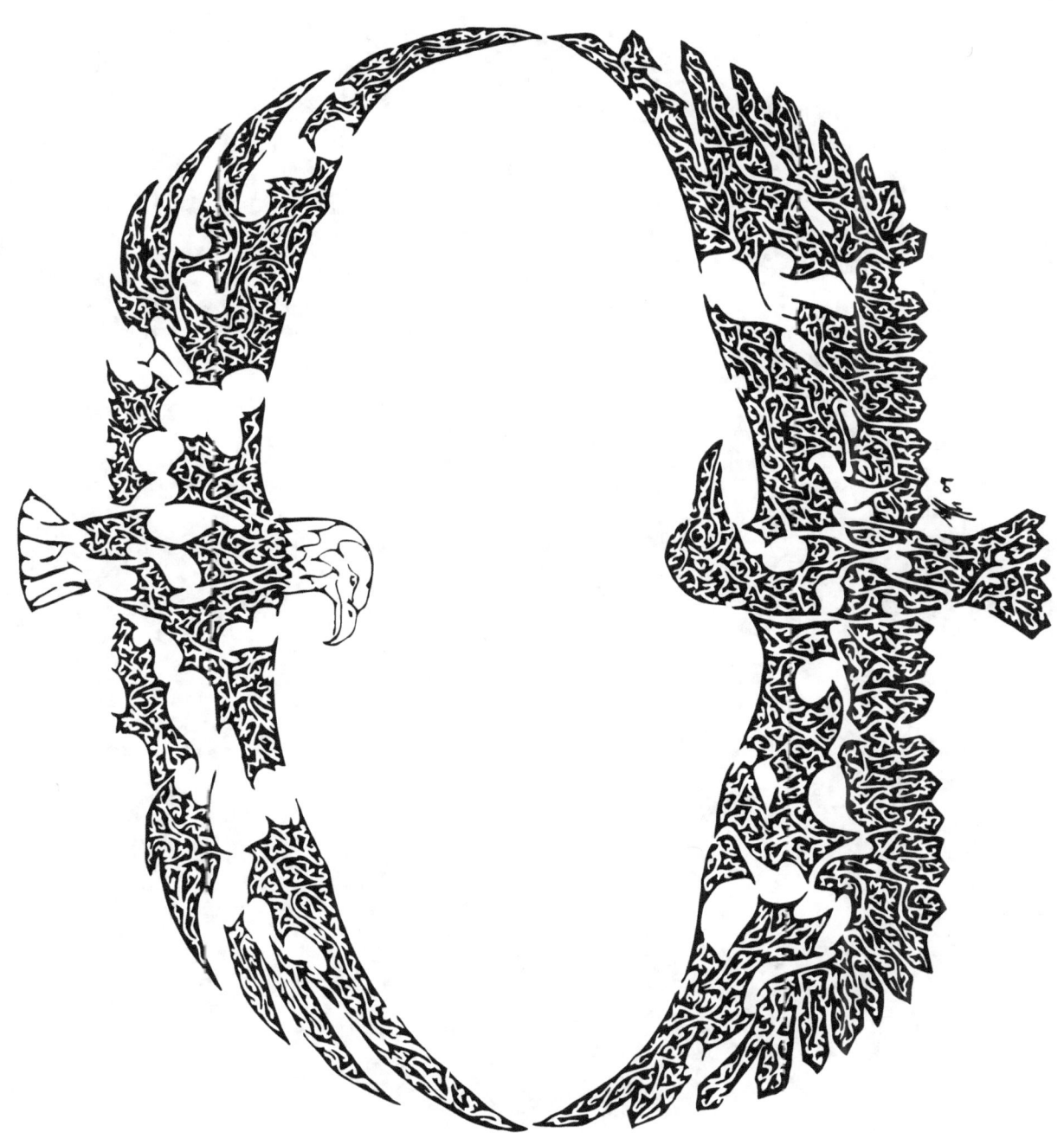

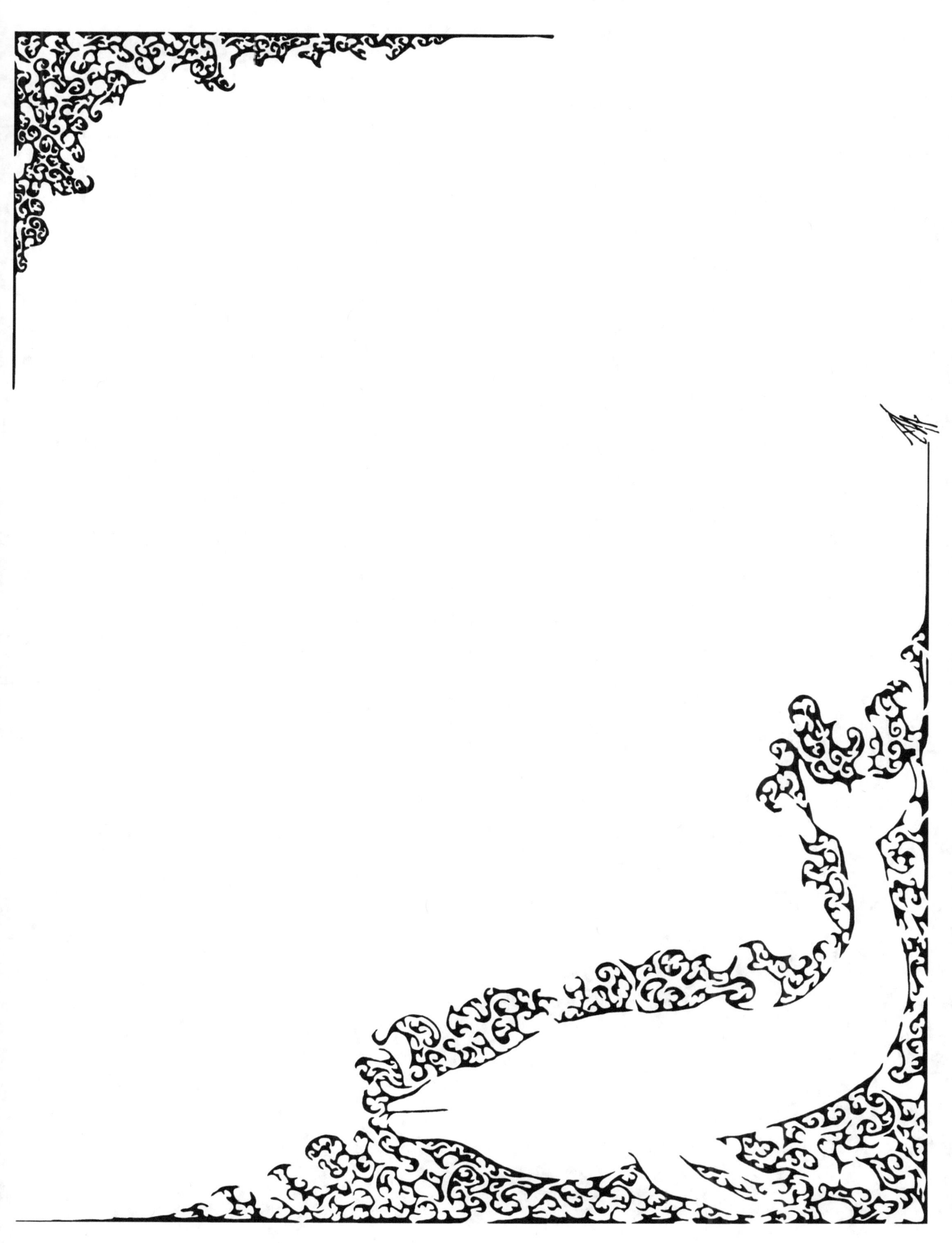

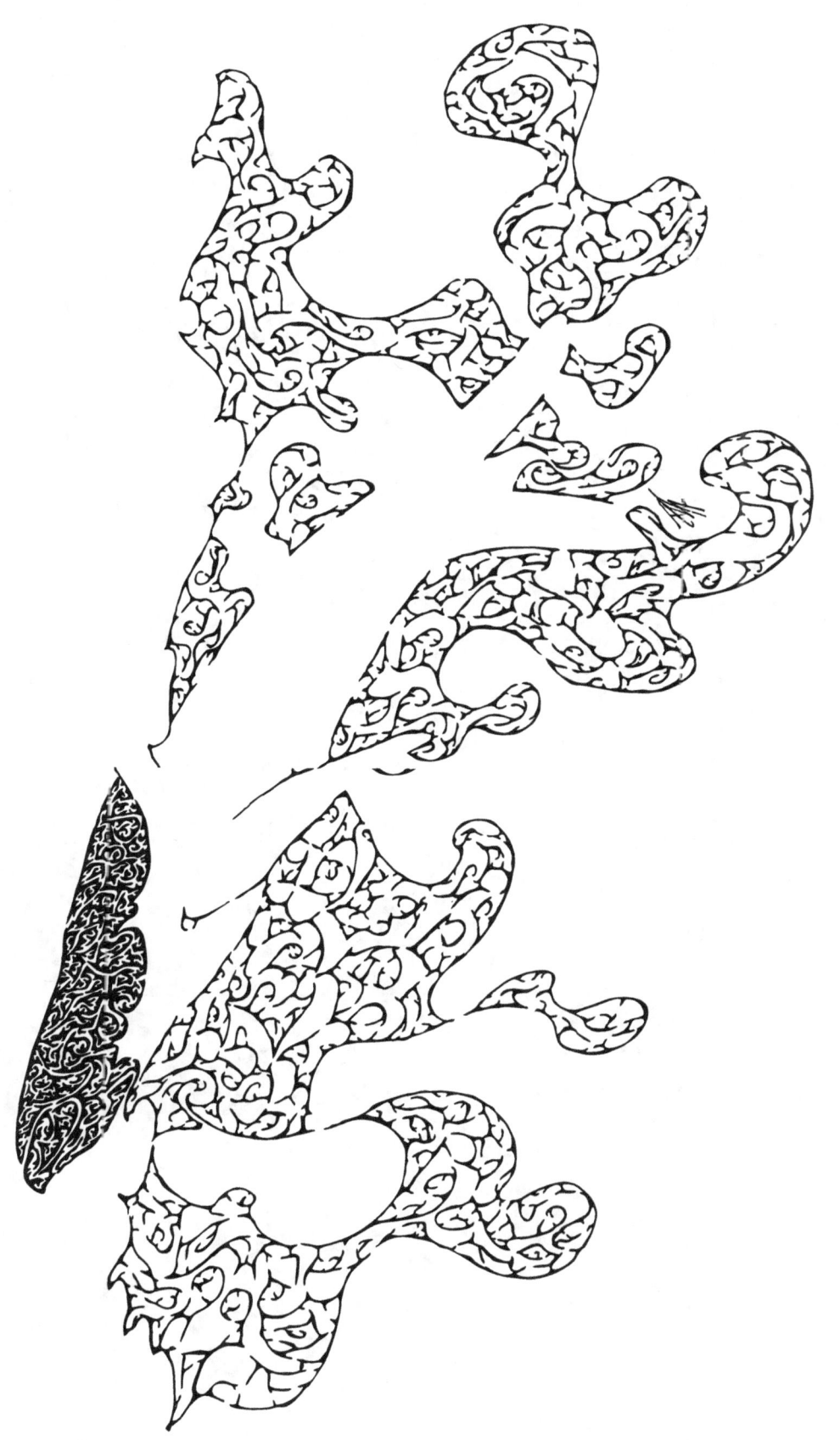

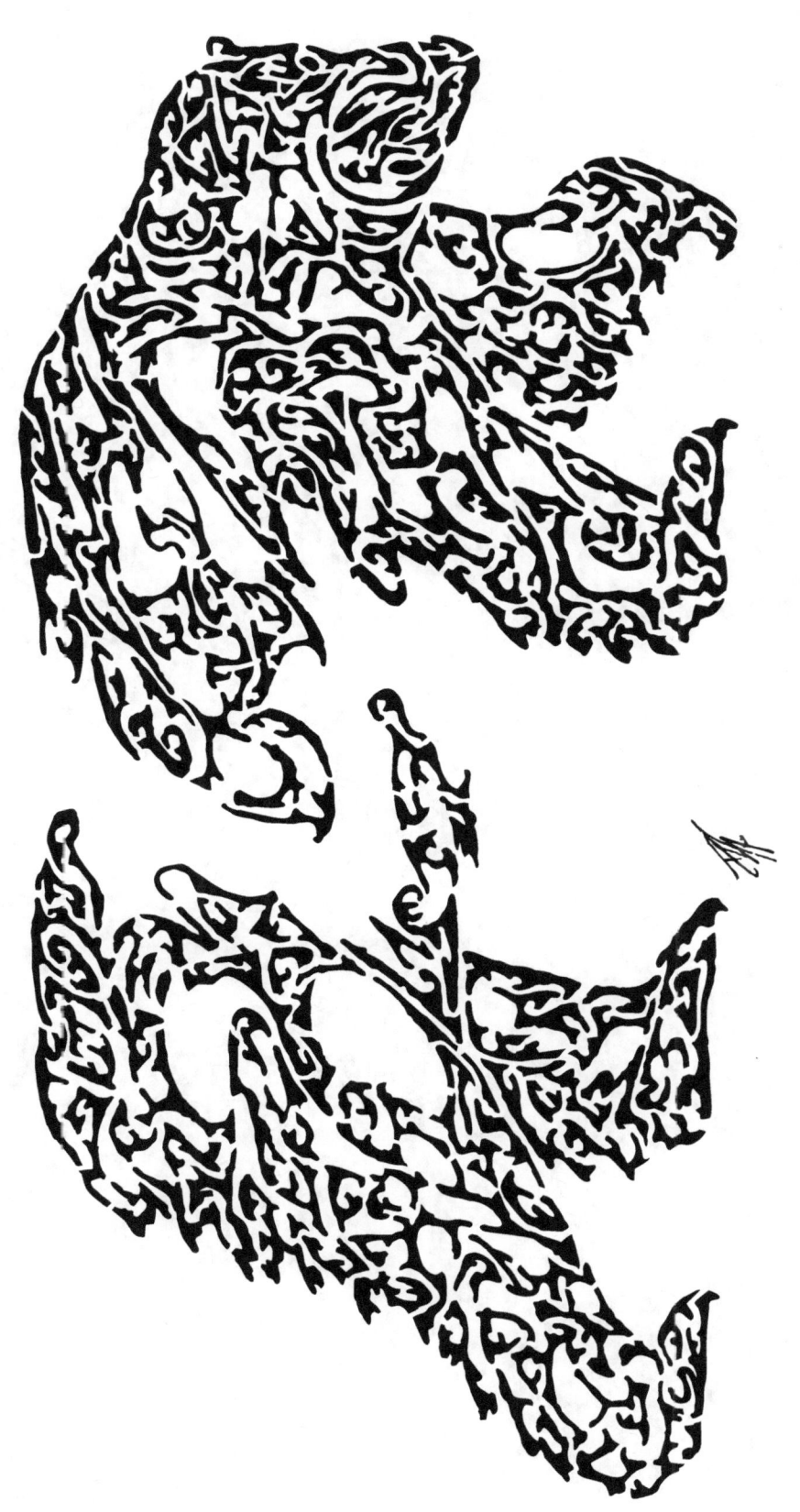

The testing page. The more watery the media
the more it will bleed thru the paper.

ALASKA INSPIRED ART

Adult Coloring book by Brian Scott

Volume 1

The testing page. The more watery the media the more it will bleed thru the paper.

Sea Turtle

Dolfins

Bold Eagle & Crow

Bear

Part of the:
Inspired Art
Coloring
Books
Series

by Brian Scott

Crow

Humpback whale diving

Wolf

Eagle in flight

Raven

Raven in tree
5 hidden faces

3 humpback whales

Bear

Eagle in flight

Sea Otto

Eagle in flight

Humpback whale

King Crab

Seal swimming backwards
stomach up head out of water

Bear

Bold Eagle

Female Orca

King Crab

Humpback
whale

Bear

Enjoy more of my art in my other coloring books

ALASKA INSPIRED ART

Adult Coloring book by Brian Scott

Volume 2

ANIMAL INSPIRED ART

Volume 3

Adult Coloring book by Brian Scott

www.ingramcontent.com/pod-product-compliance
Lightning Source LLC
Chambersburg PA
CBHW081422280526
45788CB00009B/3201